Name

Address

Blank Classic

Graph Paper Notebook
      (*Back to School*)
97 numbered pages - 100 total pages
Large 8.5 X 11

Design © 2021 Blank Classic

Blank Classic

Mailing address:
Blank Classic
PO BOX 4608
Main Station Terminal
349 West Georgia Street
Vancouver, BC
Canada, V6B 4A1

Cover design by: Lauren Dick
Interior design by: Lauren Dick

ISBN: 978-1-77476-198-4

FIRST EDITION / FIRST PRINTING

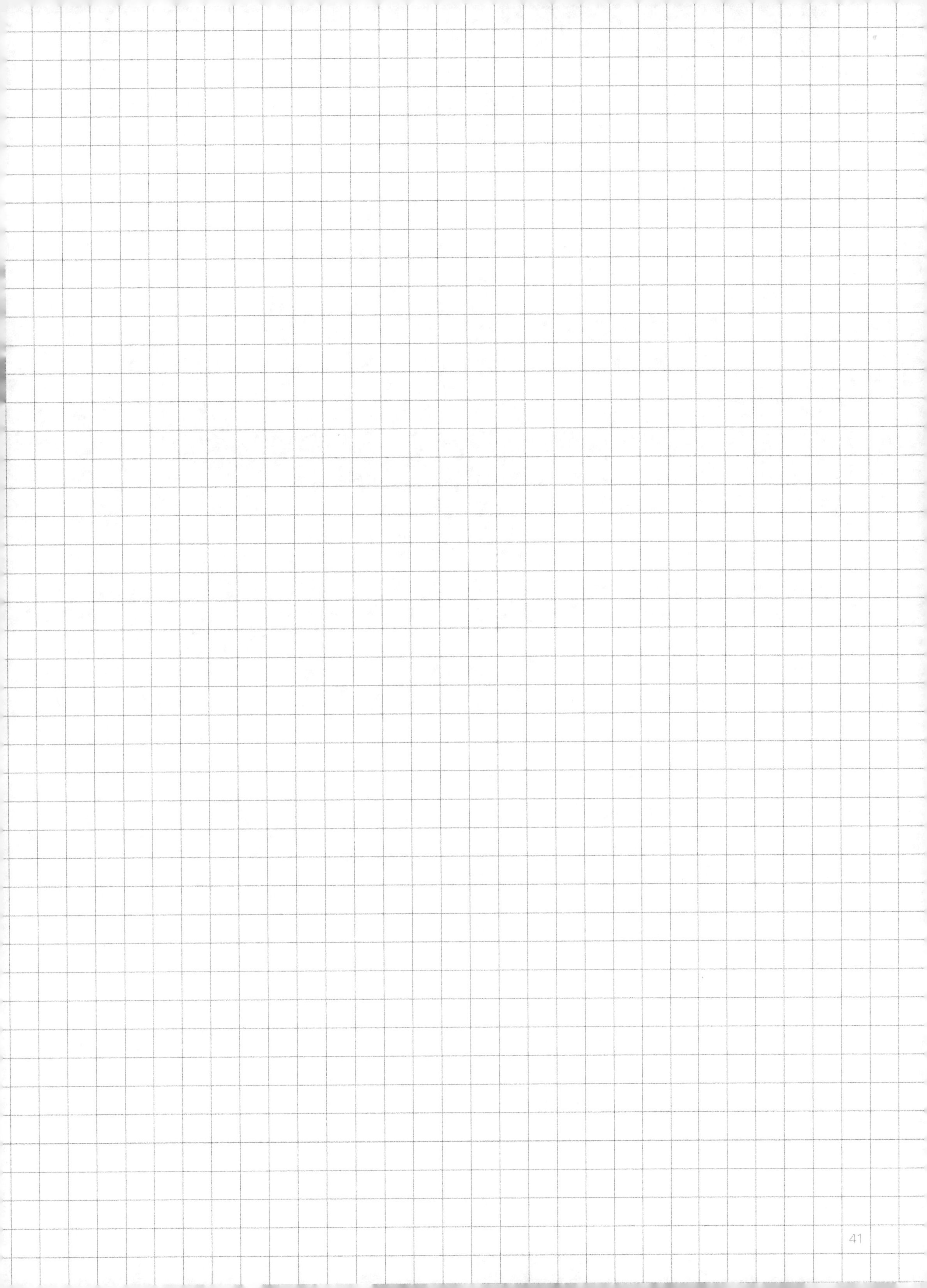

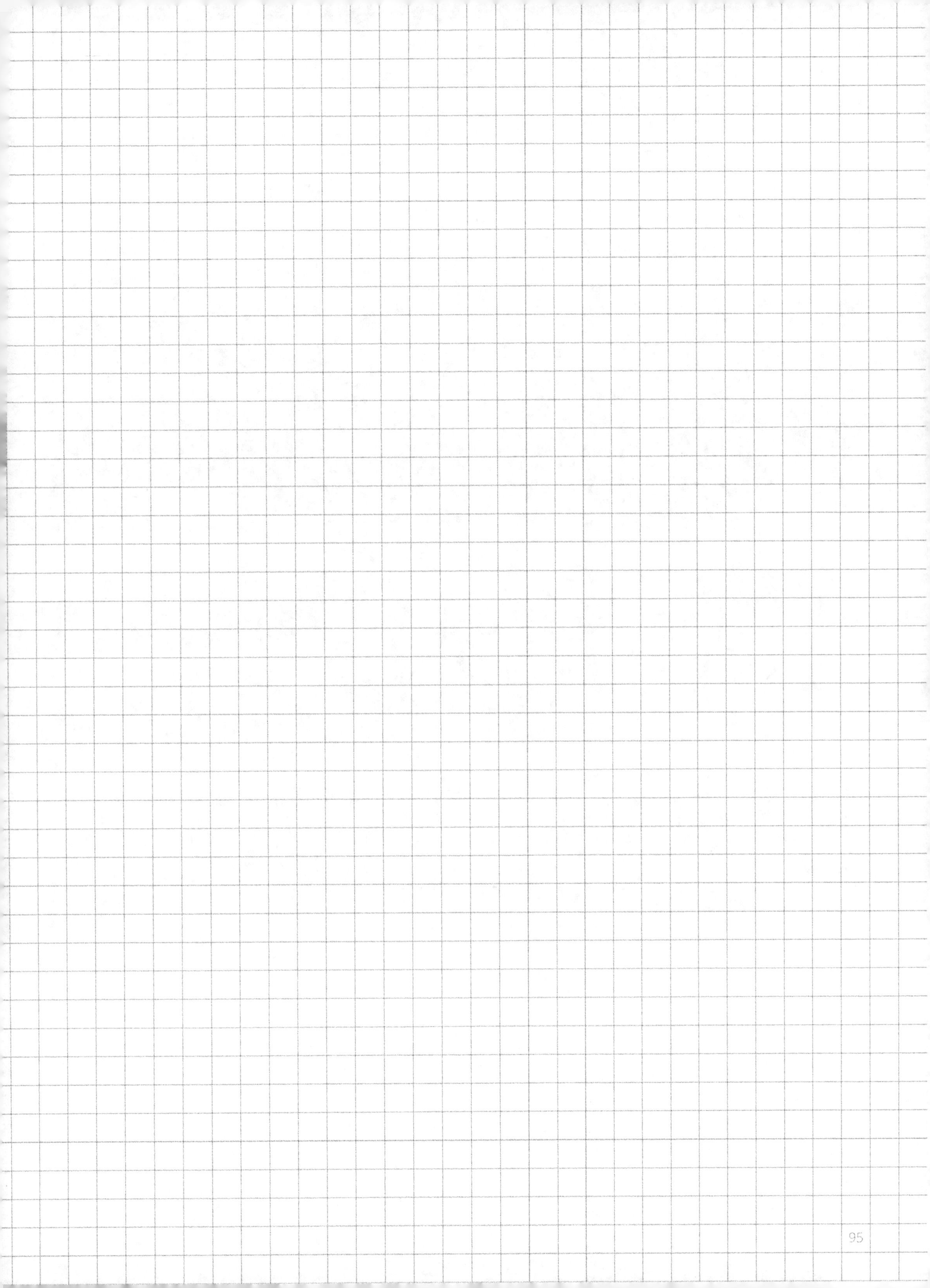

www.ingramcontent.com/pod-product-compliance
Lightning Source LLC
Chambersburg PA
CBHW080306030726
47593CB00009B/2652